# How Not to be the Perfect Wife

This is a STAR FIRE book

STAR FIRE
Crabtree Hall, Crabtree Lane
Fulham, London SW6 6TY
United Kingdom

www.star-fire.co.uk

First published 2007

07 09 11 10 08

1 3 5 7 9 10 8 6 4 2

Star Fire is part of The Foundry Creative Media Company Limited

The CIP record for this book is available from the British Library.

ISBN: 978 1 84451 940 8

Printed in China

Thanks to: Cat Emslie, Chelsea Edwards, Andy Frostick,
Victoria Lyle, Sara Robson, Nick Wells

# How Not to be the Perfect

# Wife

*Ulysses Brave*

**STAR FIRE**

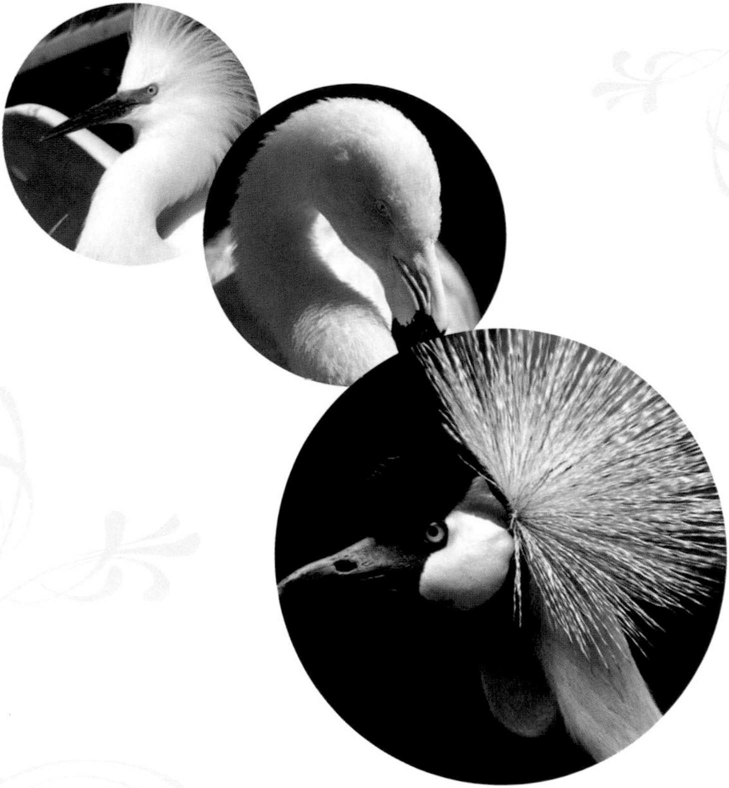

# *Foreword*

There are so many rules today, scrupulously compiled by faceless committees of governing and busy bodies. Over the years many people have appealed to me for clarity and purpose on such matters. They say that it is difficult to know how to behave in modern society, so I have penned some careful advice based on simple, old-fashioned common sense.

*Ulysses Brave*

*Be coy, but available.*

*Exercise is a critical part of your appeal to your husband. Make sure you keep in shape at all times.*

During the day it is important
to take mini-breaks from the
cleaning and scrubbing.

*Always be happy to see your husband when he comes home from a hard day's work.*

*A weekly trip to the hairdresser will keep your tail feathers ready for action, whenever your husband should choose.*

*If you stay up all night ironing, make sure that you tidy the kitchen in time for breakfast.*

*Make time in the morning to dry your underarm deodorant before waking the rest of the family.*

*Always swap anecdotes with your neighbours, they often have useful tidbits of advice.*

*If he asks for a particular food, immediately rush to find it, either from the kitchen, or if needs must, the local superstore.*

*Be careful of the latest diets.*
*They do not always produce the*
*most attractive results.*

# He'll never notice...

*Make sure you rush home to greet your husband. He will expect you to remove his coat when he arrives and minister to his various needs.*

Don't be disappointed if your husband does not notice your new skin colour. Sometimes this can be an advantage.

*Take every opportunity to check your make-up. As he opens the car door on his return from work, take a last-minute glance in the wing-mirror.*

You should allow your new hairdo to settle down before revealing it to your anxious husband.

*Never question the decisions or judgements of your husband. His word is, rightly, Law.*

Be aware of the competition.
The women at your husband's
office will find him as
commanding as you do.

*If you have worries or concerns, don't bother your husband with them, undoubtedly he will have bigger problems to think about.*

*No treatment is too expensive or painful in the righteous attempt to please your husband.*

*Feel free to indulge in a bit of pampering in the queue to pick up your husband's dry-cleaning.*

*Housemaid's knee is common for the perfect wife and husbands will understand that it occasionally restricts mobility.*

*Try not to show to your husband your exhaustion from daily chores.*

*Wifely duties might also include the need to conduct a 48-piece orchestra to celebrate your husband's latest big deal.*

*If your husband likes to play the field, try not to let it upset you.*

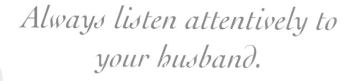

*Always listen attentively to your husband.*

When shopping for your family,
you might need to fight your
way to the till.

*Try also to find a treat for your husband that he will enjoy when he returns from the pub.*

*If your husband waits in the car while you do the shopping he may become suspicious if you flirt with supermarket personnel.*

Bending over in front of your neighbours is guaranteed to keep your husband on his toes.

*Husbands often need time to themselves. Be prepared to leave your own house for a few hours, however late.*

*If your husband comes home late,*
*try to understand his needs and*
*remain alert when he returns.*

*Before your husband comes down for breakfast, make sure that the children know their tasks and understand the need for silence.*

*Try to convince yourself that the only true rival for your husband's affection is your own reflection.*

*Always remain humble in the presence of your husband. Remember, his needs are greater than your own.*

*Come back soon!*